Table of Contents

Chapter 1: Introduction to AI Trends for the Next Decade 2

Chapter 2: Understanding the Current Landscape of AI 5

Chapter 3: Predicting AI Trends for the Next Decade 9

Chapter 4: Expert Insights on AI Trends 14

Chapter 5: Implementing AI Trends in Your Business 17

Chapter 6: Looking Towards the Future of AI 21

Chapter 7: Conclusion and Key Takeaways 25

AI Trends 29

Leading Companies That Are at The Forefront of AI Innovation And Revolutionizing The Field: 34

Chapter 1: Introduction to AI Trends for the Next Decade

The Growing Importance of AI and Data Science

As we move further into the 21st century, the importance of artificial intelligence (AI) and data science is becoming increasingly evident across various industries. AI and data science are revolutionizing the way businesses operate, leading to more efficient processes, better decision-making, and improved customer experiences. For innovators looking to stay ahead of the curve, understanding and harnessing the power of AI and data science is essential.

AI experts and data science professionals are at the forefront of this technological revolution, constantly pushing the boundaries of what is possible with data. They are exploring new algorithms, tools, and techniques to extract valuable insights from vast amounts of data, enabling businesses to make informed decisions and drive innovation. The insights generated by these experts are driving advancements in fields such as healthcare, finance, manufacturing, and more.

One of the key trends that AI experts and data science pros are predicting for the next decade is the continued integration of AI into everyday life. From virtual assistants and smart homes to autonomous vehicles and personalized recommendations, AI is becoming increasingly pervasive in our lives. This trend is expected to accelerate in the coming years, as AI technologies become more sophisticated and accessible to a wider range of industries.

Another important trend that AI experts and data science pros are focused on is the ethical implications of AI and data science. As AI systems become more advanced, questions about privacy, bias, and transparency are becoming more pressing. AI experts are working to address these concerns by developing ethical guidelines and frameworks to ensure that AI technologies are used responsibly and ethically.

In conclusion, the growing importance of AI and data science cannot be overstated. For innovators looking to make an impact in their industries, understanding and leveraging AI and data science is crucial. By staying informed about the latest trends and developments in AI and data science, innovators can position themselves at the forefront of this technological revolution and drive meaningful change in their respective fields.

Overview of Predictive Analytics and Machine Learning

In the subchapter "Overview of Predictive Analytics and Machine Learning" from the book "Data Science Decoded: Predicting AI Trends for the Next Decade," we delve into the fundamental concepts of predictive analytics and machine learning. Predictive analytics involves using historical data to predict future outcomes, while machine learning is a subset of artificial intelligence that focuses on developing algorithms that enable computers to learn from data and make predictions without being explicitly programmed.

For innovators in the field of data science and artificial intelligence, understanding predictive analytics and machine learning is essential for staying ahead of the curve. By leveraging these technologies, businesses can gain valuable insights into customer behavior, market trends, and potential risks, allowing them to make informed decisions and drive innovation.

AI experts and data science professionals agree that predictive analytics and machine learning will play a crucial role in shaping the future of AI trends in the next decade. With advancements in technology and the increasing availability of data, these tools will continue to evolve and become more sophisticated, enabling companies to unlock new opportunities and drive growth.

The combination of predictive analytics and machine learning has already revolutionized industries such as healthcare, finance, and e-commerce, enabling companies to streamline operations, improve efficiency, and deliver personalized experiences to customers. As we look towards the future, these technologies will only become more prevalent and impactful, driving further innovation and reshaping the way businesses operate.

In conclusion, a solid understanding of predictive analytics and machine learning is essential for innovators looking to harness the power of data science and artificial intelligence in the coming decade. By staying informed about the latest trends and advancements in these technologies, businesses can position themselves for success and unlock new opportunities for growth and innovation.

Chapter 2: Understanding the Current Landscape of AI

Applications of AI in Various Industries

In recent years, the application of artificial intelligence (AI) has revolutionized various industries, driving innovation and efficiency in ways previously unimaginable. From healthcare to finance, AI has been leveraged to streamline processes, enhance decision-making, and improve overall outcomes. In this chapter, we will explore some of the key applications of AI in various industries, shedding light on the transformative power of this technology.

One industry that has seen significant advancements through the integration of AI is healthcare. With the ability to analyze vast amounts of data and identify patterns that may not be apparent to human clinicians, AI has been instrumental in diagnosing diseases, predicting patient outcomes, and personalizing treatment plans. From medical imaging to drug discovery, AI is revolutionizing the way healthcare is delivered, ultimately leading to better patient care and improved health outcomes.

In the finance industry, AI has played a crucial role in enhancing risk management, fraud detection, and customer service. By analyzing market trends in real-time, AI-powered algorithms can make more accurate predictions, enabling financial institutions to make informed decisions and mitigate risks. Additionally, AI chatbots have transformed customer service, providing personalized and efficient support to clients while reducing operational costs for businesses.

In the transportation sector, AI has been instrumental in improving safety, efficiency, and sustainability. Through the use of AI-powered algorithms, autonomous vehicles can navigate roads, detect obstacles, and make split-second decisions to avoid accidents. Furthermore, AI has been used to optimize traffic flow, reduce congestion, and minimize carbon emissions, making transportation systems more efficient and environmentally friendly.

In the retail industry, AI has been leveraged to enhance customer experience, optimize supply chain management, and drive sales. By analyzing customer data and behavior, AI can provide personalized product recommendations, improve inventory management, and predict future trends. Additionally, AI-powered chatbots and virtual assistants have transformed the way retailers interact with customers, providing instant support and enhancing customer satisfaction. Overall, the applications of AI in various industries are limitless, offering endless opportunities for innovation and growth in the years to come.

Key Players in the AI Space

When it comes to the world of artificial intelligence, there are several key players who are leading the way in innovation and shaping the future of the industry. These companies and individuals are at the forefront of developing cutting-edge technology and pushing the boundaries of what is possible with AI.

One of the most well-known players in the AI space is Google. With their deep pockets and access to vast amounts of data, Google has been able to make significant advancements in AI research and development. From self-driving cars to natural language processing, Google is constantly pushing the boundaries of what AI can do.

Another key player in the AI space is IBM. With their Watson platform, IBM has been able to leverage AI technology to help businesses across a variety of industries make more informed decisions and improve their operations. IBM is also heavily involved in research and development, constantly working to push the boundaries of what is possible with AI.

In addition to companies like Google and IBM, there are also several key individuals who are making a significant impact in the AI space. One such individual is Andrew Ng, a renowned AI researcher and cofounder of Google Brain. Ng has been instrumental in advancing AI technology and has been a leading voice in the industry for many years.

Overall, the key players in the AI space are driving innovation and shaping the future of the industry. Whether it's through groundbreaking research, cutting-edge technology, or visionary leadership, these individuals and companies are at the forefront of the AI revolution and are helping to define what AI will look like in the next decade.

Chapter 3: Predicting AI Trends for the Next Decade
The Rise of Explainable AI

As we enter a new era of artificial intelligence (AI), one of the most significant trends that experts are predicting is the rise of explainable AI. This shift in focus is driven by the need for transparency and accountability in AI systems, as well as the growing awareness of the potential risks associated with opaque algorithms.

Explainable AI refers to the ability of AI systems to provide clear explanations for their decisions and actions. This is crucial for ensuring that users can trust and understand the outputs of AI systems, especially in high-stakes applications such as healthcare, finance, and autonomous vehicles. By making AI more transparent and interpretable, we can improve its reliability and reduce the potential for bias and errors.

One of the key drivers behind the rise of explainable AI is the increasing regulatory scrutiny around AI systems. Governments and regulatory bodies are starting to require that AI systems provide explanations for their decisions, particularly in sectors where the impact of AI can have significant consequences on individuals and society as a whole. This trend is pushing organizations to prioritize transparency and interpretability in their AI development processes.

In addition to regulatory pressures, there is also a growing demand from users and stakeholders for AI systems that are more transparent and explainable. As AI becomes more integrated into our daily lives, people are becoming more aware of the potential risks and limitations of AI systems. By making AI more explainable, organizations can build trust with their users and demonstrate a commitment to ethical and responsible AI development.

Overall, the rise of explainable AI represents a significant shift in the AI landscape, with implications for both the development and deployment of AI systems. By prioritizing transparency and interpretability, organizations can build more trustworthy and reliable AI systems that meet the needs and expectations of users and regulators alike. As we look towards the next decade, it is clear that explainable AI will play a crucial role in shaping the future of AI and data science.

Ethical Considerations in AI Development

Ethical considerations in AI development are crucial for ensuring that artificial intelligence technologies are used responsibly and ethically. As AI continues to advance and become more integrated into various aspects of society, it is important for innovators to consider the potential ethical implications of their work. This includes issues such as bias in AI algorithms, data privacy, and the impact of AI on job displacement.

One of the key ethical considerations in AI development is bias in algorithms. AI systems are only as good as the data they are trained on, and if this data is biased, it can lead to biased outcomes. For example, if an AI algorithm is trained on data that is predominantly from one demographic group, it may not perform as well for other groups. This can lead to unfair or discriminatory outcomes, which can have serious implications for individuals and society as a whole.

Data privacy is another important ethical consideration in AI development. As AI technologies collect and analyze large amounts of data, there is the potential for personal information to be misused or compromised. Innovators must take steps to ensure that data is collected and stored securely, and that individuals have control over how their data is used. This includes obtaining informed consent from individuals before collecting their data, and implementing robust security measures to protect data from unauthorized access.

The impact of AI on job displacement is also a significant ethical consideration. As AI technologies become more advanced, there is the potential for automation to replace human workers in various industries. This can lead to job loss and economic disruption, particularly for workers in low-skilled or routine jobs. Innovators must consider the ethical implications of this trend and work to mitigate its impact, such as by investing in retraining programs for displaced workers or exploring new job opportunities created by AI.

In conclusion, ethical considerations in AI development are essential for ensuring that artificial intelligence technologies are used in a responsible and ethical manner. By addressing issues such as bias in algorithms, data privacy, and the impact of AI on job displacement, innovators can help to create a more equitable and sustainable future for AI. It is important for AI experts and data science professionals to engage with these ethical considerations and work towards developing AI technologies that benefit society as a whole.

Impact of AI on the Future of Work

The impact of artificial intelligence on the future of work is a topic that has generated significant interest among innovators in the field of data science and AI. As we look ahead to the next decade, it is clear that AI will continue to play a transformative role in the way we work and the skills that will be in demand. According to AI experts and data science professionals, the integration of AI into various industries will lead to both opportunities and challenges for workers.

One of the key ways in which AI is expected to impact the future of work is through automation. As AI technology becomes more advanced, tasks that were previously performed by humans will increasingly be automated, leading to changes in the types of jobs that are available. While this may result in the displacement of some workers, it also has the potential to create new opportunities in fields such as data science, machine learning, and AI development.

Another important aspect of AI's impact on the future of work is the need for workers to adapt and acquire new skills. As AI technology continues to evolve, there will be a growing demand for workers who are proficient in data analysis, machine learning, and other AI-related skills. This presents both a challenge and an opportunity for workers to upskill and stay relevant in the evolving job market.

Furthermore, the integration of AI into various industries is expected to lead to increased productivity and efficiency. By leveraging AI technologies, businesses will be able to streamline processes, make data-driven decisions, and create new products and services that were previously not possible. This has the potential to drive economic growth and create new job opportunities in emerging fields related to AI.

In conclusion, the impact of AI on the future of work is a complex and multifaceted issue that will require collaboration between workers, businesses, and policymakers to navigate successfully. By staying informed about AI trends and investing in the necessary skills and training, workers can position themselves for success in the rapidly changing job market. As we look ahead to the next decade, it is clear that AI will continue to shape the future of work in ways that we are only beginning to understand.

Chapter 4: Expert Insights on AI Trends
Interviews with Leading AI Experts

In this subchapter, we delve into interviews with leading AI experts to gain insights into the future trends of artificial intelligence. These experts have dedicated their careers to understanding and advancing the field of AI, making them valuable sources of information for innovators looking to stay ahead of the curve.

One key theme that emerged from our interviews is the increasing focus on ethical AI. As AI systems become more powerful and pervasive, experts are calling for greater attention to the ethical implications of their use. This includes considerations of bias, transparency, and accountability in AI algorithms, as well as the impact of AI on society as a whole.

Another trend that experts highlighted is the growing importance of interpretability in AI models. As AI systems become more complex and opaque, the ability to understand and interpret their decisions becomes essential for ensuring their reliability and trustworthiness. Experts are working on developing new techniques and tools to make AI models more interpretable and explainable.

Experts also pointed to the rise of AI-powered automation as a major trend for the next decade. As AI technology continues to advance, more and more tasks and processes will be automated, leading to significant changes in the workforce and economy. Experts emphasized the need for policymakers and businesses to prepare for the impact of automation on jobs and society.

Overall, the interviews with leading AI experts provide valuable insights into the future of artificial intelligence. By understanding the trends and challenges that lie ahead, innovators can better prepare for the opportunities and risks that AI will bring in the next decade. The expertise and perspectives of these experts are essential for shaping the future of AI in a way that benefits society as a whole.

Surveys and Studies on AI Trends

In the realm of artificial intelligence (AI), staying ahead of the curve is crucial for innovators looking to make a lasting impact. Surveys and studies on AI trends provide valuable insights into what the future holds for this rapidly evolving field. By examining the thoughts and predictions of AI experts and data science professionals, we can gain a clearer understanding of where the industry is headed in the next decade.

One prevalent trend that has emerged from recent surveys is the increasing focus on ethical AI. As AI technologies become more advanced and integrated into various aspects of our lives, concerns about bias, privacy, and accountability have come to the forefront. Experts are calling for greater transparency and regulation to ensure that AI is developed and deployed responsibly.

Another key trend that has been identified is the rise of AI in healthcare. From predictive analytics to personalized medicine, AI is revolutionizing the way healthcare providers diagnose, treat, and care for patients. With the potential to improve outcomes and reduce costs, the healthcare industry is poised to benefit greatly from advancements in AI technology.

In addition to healthcare, AI is also making waves in industries such as finance, marketing, and transportation. As businesses seek to gain a competitive edge, they are increasingly turning to AI to optimize processes, enhance customer experiences, and drive innovation. By leveraging the power of AI, companies can unlock new opportunities for growth and success in the digital age.

Overall, surveys and studies on AI trends provide valuable insights for innovators looking to navigate the ever-changing landscape of data science and artificial intelligence. By staying informed and proactive, we can anticipate upcoming trends, adapt to new technologies, and position ourselves for success in the next decade and beyond. As we continue to push the boundaries of what is possible with AI, the opportunities for innovation and discovery are truly limitless.

Chapter 5: Implementing AI Trends in Your Business
Strategies for Incorporating AI into Your Business

Incorporating artificial intelligence (AI) into your business can have a transformative impact on your operations, customer experience, and overall success. As AI technologies continue to evolve at a rapid pace, it is becoming increasingly important for businesses to stay ahead of the curve and leverage these tools effectively. In this subchapter, we will explore some key strategies for incorporating AI into your business to help you unlock its full potential and drive innovation.

One of the first steps in integrating AI into your business is to identify the areas where AI can have the most impact. This could include automating repetitive tasks, improving decision-making processes, enhancing customer service, or optimizing supply chain operations. By understanding the specific challenges and opportunities within your organization, you can better tailor your AI strategy to address these needs and drive measurable results.

Once you have identified the areas where AI can add value, it is important to invest in the right technology and talent to support your AI initiatives. This may involve partnering with AI vendors, hiring data scientists and AI experts, or training your existing workforce on AI technologies. By building a strong foundation of AI capabilities within your organization, you can ensure that you are well-equipped to leverage these tools effectively and drive business growth.

In addition to investing in technology and talent, it is crucial to establish clear goals and metrics for your AI initiatives. By defining key performance indicators (KPIs) and setting measurable targets for your AI projects, you can track progress, evaluate success, and make data-driven decisions to drive continuous improvement. This will help ensure that your AI investments are aligned with your business objectives and are delivering tangible value to your organization.

Finally, it is important to continuously monitor and optimize your AI initiatives to ensure ongoing success. This may involve conducting regular performance reviews, gathering feedback from stakeholders, and iterating on your AI solutions to address any issues or challenges that arise. By adopting a proactive approach to AI implementation and management, you can position your business for long-term success and stay ahead of the competition in the ever-evolving AI landscape.

Overcoming Challenges in Adopting AI Technologies

In the rapidly evolving landscape of artificial intelligence (AI) technologies, innovators are faced with a myriad of challenges when it comes to adopting these cutting-edge tools. One of the main hurdles that organizations encounter is the lack of understanding and expertise in implementing AI solutions. Many companies struggle to find the right talent with the necessary skills to develop and deploy AI systems effectively. This shortage of skilled professionals can hinder the adoption of AI technologies and slow down the pace of innovation in various industries.

Another obstacle that innovators face is the high cost associated with implementing AI technologies. Developing AI solutions requires significant investment in infrastructure, tools, and resources. Additionally, the ongoing maintenance and updates of AI systems can add to the financial burden. For many organizations, the cost of adopting AI technologies can be prohibitive, especially for smaller businesses or startups. Finding ways to overcome these financial barriers is essential for ensuring widespread adoption of AI technologies across different sectors.

Data privacy and security concerns also pose significant challenges for organizations looking to adopt AI technologies. With the increasing amount of data being collected and analyzed by AI systems, there is a growing concern about the potential misuse or exploitation of sensitive information. Ensuring the privacy and security of data is crucial for building trust with customers and stakeholders. Addressing these concerns requires implementing robust data protection measures and compliance with regulations such as GDPR and CCPA.

The complexity of AI technologies and their integration with existing systems is another challenge that innovators must navigate. AI solutions often require integration with different software platforms, databases, and APIs, which can be a complex and time-consuming process. Ensuring seamless integration and interoperability between AI systems and existing infrastructure is essential for maximizing the benefits of AI technologies. Overcoming these technical challenges requires careful planning, collaboration between different teams, and a deep understanding of the underlying technologies.

Despite the challenges that innovators face in adopting AI technologies, there are opportunities for growth and innovation in the coming decade. By addressing the talent shortage, investing in the right resources, prioritizing data privacy and security, and focusing on seamless integration, organizations can overcome these challenges and unlock the full potential of AI technologies. With the right strategies and a forward-thinking mindset, innovators can harness the power of AI to drive transformative changes in various industries and shape the future of data science.

Chapter 6: Looking Towards the Future of AI
Emerging Technologies in AI

As we look towards the future of artificial intelligence (AI), it is important to consider the emerging technologies that are shaping the landscape of data science and predictive analytics. From machine learning to deep learning, AI experts and data science professionals are constantly exploring new tools and techniques to improve the accuracy and efficiency of AI systems.

One of the most exciting trends in AI is the rise of reinforcement learning, a type of machine learning that enables AI systems to learn from their interactions with the environment. This technology has been used to develop autonomous vehicles, optimize supply chain operations, and even play complex games like Go. As we enter the next decade, we can expect to see even more applications of reinforcement learning in various industries.

Another key technology that is gaining traction in the AI space is natural language processing (NLP). NLP allows machines to understand and generate human language, opening up new possibilities for chatbots, virtual assistants, and language translation services. With advancements in NLP, we can anticipate more sophisticated AI applications that can communicate and interact with humans in a more natural and intuitive way.

Furthermore, the integration of AI and the Internet of Things (IoT) is revolutionizing how we collect and analyze data. By connecting smart devices to AI systems, we can unlock valuable insights from vast amounts of sensor data. This convergence of AI and IoT has the potential to transform industries such as healthcare, manufacturing, and agriculture, paving the way for more efficient and automated processes.

In conclusion, the future of AI is bright with a plethora of emerging technologies that are reshaping the way we approach data science and predictive analytics. By staying informed and embracing these advancements, innovators in the field of AI can leverage these tools to develop cutting-edge solutions that will drive the next wave of technological innovation. The possibilities are endless, and the next decade promises to be an exciting time for AI professionals and researchers alike.

Predictions for the Next Decade of AI Development

As we look ahead to the next decade of AI development, there are several predictions that experts in the field are making. One key trend that is expected to continue is the increasing use of AI in everyday life. From virtual assistants to self-driving cars, AI technology is becoming more integrated into our daily routines. Innovators can expect to see even more AI-powered products and services in the coming years.

Another prediction for the next decade is the continued growth of machine learning algorithms. These algorithms are at the core of many AI applications, and advancements in this area are expected to drive further innovation. As data science professionals work to improve the accuracy and efficiency of these algorithms, we can expect to see even more powerful AI systems emerge.

One area that is expected to see significant growth in the next decade is natural language processing (NLP). With the rise of voice assistants and chatbots, NLP technology is becoming increasingly important. Innovators can expect to see continued advancements in this area, with AI becoming even more adept at understanding and generating human language.

In addition to these trends, experts predict that AI ethics and regulation will become increasingly important in the next decade. As AI technology becomes more pervasive, questions about privacy, bias, and accountability will need to be addressed. Data science professionals will need to work closely with policymakers and ethicists to ensure that AI is developed and deployed responsibly.

Overall, the next decade of AI development promises to be an exciting time for innovators in the field. With advancements in machine learning, natural language processing, and ethics, there is no doubt that AI will continue to shape the way we live and work. By staying informed and proactive, data science professionals can help to drive these trends forward in a positive and impactful way.

Chapter 7: Conclusion and Key Takeaways
Recap of AI Trends for the Next Decade

As we look towards the future of artificial intelligence (AI) in the next decade, it is important to recap some of the current trends that are shaping this rapidly evolving field. AI experts and data science professionals have been closely monitoring the developments in AI technology and have identified several key trends that are expected to dominate the landscape in the coming years.

One of the most significant trends in AI is the rise of machine learning algorithms. These algorithms have revolutionized the way we approach data analysis and have opened up new possibilities for automation and predictive modeling. Machine learning algorithms are being used in a wide range of applications, from self-driving cars to personalized marketing campaigns, and are expected to continue to drive innovation in the field of AI in the years to come.

Another important trend in AI is the increasing focus on ethical considerations and bias in AI algorithms. As AI technology becomes more pervasive in our daily lives, there is a growing awareness of the potential risks and pitfalls associated with biased algorithms. AI experts and data science professionals are working to develop more transparent and fair AI systems that can be trusted to make unbiased decisions.

In addition to machine learning and ethical considerations, AI experts are also closely monitoring the development of deep learning technology. Deep learning algorithms are a subset of machine learning algorithms that are capable of learning from large amounts of data and making complex decisions. Deep learning technology is being used in a wide range of applications, from natural language processing to image recognition, and is expected to play a key role in the future of AI.

Overall, the future of AI looks bright, with exciting opportunities for innovation and growth in the coming decade. By staying informed about the latest trends and developments in the field of AI, innovators can position themselves to take advantage of the opportunities that lie ahead and drive the next wave of AI innovation.

Actionable Steps for Innovators in the AI Space

In the rapidly evolving field of artificial intelligence, it is crucial for innovators to stay ahead of the curve and anticipate future trends. To help you navigate the ever-changing landscape of AI, here are some actionable steps that you can take to position yourself for success in the next decade.

1. Stay informed: One of the most important things you can do as an innovator in the AI space is to stay informed about the latest developments and trends. This means keeping up to date with new research, attending conferences and workshops, and networking with other professionals in the field. By staying informed, you can ensure that you are always aware of the latest advancements in AI and can position yourself as a thought leader in the industry.

2. Experiment with new technologies: As an innovator, it is important to constantly experiment with new technologies and tools in order to stay ahead of the curve. This might involve playing around with new algorithms, testing out different machine learning models, or exploring new data sources. By experimenting with new technologies, you can gain valuable insights and stay ahead of the competition.

3. Collaborate with others: Collaboration is key in the world of AI. By working with other innovators, data scientists, and AI experts, you can leverage their expertise and insights to drive innovation in your own

work. Collaborating with others can also help you to access new resources, networks, and opportunities that you might not have had access to otherwise.

4. Focus on ethical considerations: As AI becomes increasingly integrated into our everyday lives, it is important for innovators to consider the ethical implications of their work. This means thinking critically about issues such as bias, privacy, and transparency, and taking steps to ensure that your AI systems are designed and implemented in an ethical and responsible manner.

5. Think long-term: Finally, as an innovator in the AI space, it is important to think long-term and consider the future implications of your work. This might involve thinking about how your AI systems will scale as they become more widely adopted, or considering how they might impact society as a whole. By taking a long-term perspective, you can ensure that your work has a lasting impact and contributes to the advancement of the field.

AI Trends

Explainable AI (XAI):

- As AI systems become more complex, there is a growing need for models that can provide understandable explanations for their decisions. Explainable AI aims to make AI decision-making more transparent and interpretable to users.

AI Ethics and Governance:

- With the increasing deployment of AI in critical areas, there is a significant focus on developing ethical guidelines and governance frameworks to ensure AI systems are fair, accountable, and do not perpetuate biases.

Edge AI:

- Moving AI processing to the edge of networks, closer to where data is generated (e.g., IoT devices), reduces latency, enhances data privacy, and decreases bandwidth usage. This trend is driven by the need for real-time processing in applications like autonomous vehicles and smart cities.

AI in Healthcare:

- AI is transforming healthcare through applications in predictive diagnostics, personalized medicine, drug discovery, and robotic surgery. The use of AI to analyze medical data and images is improving accuracy and efficiency in patient care.

Natural Language Processing (NLP) Advancements:

- Recent breakthroughs in NLP, like OpenAI's GPT-4, are enabling more sophisticated and human-like interactions between machines and humans. These advancements are being applied in chatbots, virtual assistants, and automated content creation.

AI-Powered Automation:

- AI is driving automation across various industries, from manufacturing and logistics to customer service and finance. Intelligent automation, including robotic process automation (RPA) integrated with AI, is enhancing efficiency and reducing costs.

Federated Learning:

- This collaborative machine learning approach allows models to be trained across multiple decentralized devices or servers while maintaining data privacy. Federated learning is gaining traction in sectors like healthcare and finance, where data privacy is paramount.

AI and Cybersecurity:

- AI is playing a crucial role in enhancing cybersecurity by detecting and responding to threats in real-time. AI-driven security systems can analyze vast amounts of data to identify patterns and anomalies that indicate potential cyber-attacks.

Generative AI:

- AI models that can generate new content, such as text, images, music, and even code, are becoming more sophisticated. Generative AI has applications in entertainment, design, marketing, and more.

Quantum AI:

- The intersection of quantum computing and AI, known as quantum AI, is an emerging field that promises to solve complex problems faster than classical computers. While still in its early stages, quantum AI has potential applications in cryptography, optimization, and material science.

AI-Driven Personalization:

- AI is enhancing personalization in areas like marketing, e-commerce, and entertainment. By analyzing user data, AI systems can deliver highly tailored recommendations and experiences.

AI in Environmental Sustainability:

- AI is being leveraged to address environmental challenges, such as climate change, through applications like energy optimization, wildlife conservation, and climate modeling.

Multimodal AI:

- Combining multiple types of data (e.g., text, image, audio) to create more comprehensive and intelligent systems. Multimodal AI enables more robust and versatile applications, such as enhanced virtual assistants and comprehensive data analysis tools.

AI Democratization:

- Efforts to make AI tools and technologies more accessible to non-experts are increasing. Platforms and frameworks that simplify AI development and deployment are helping businesses and individuals harness the power of AI without needing deep technical expertise.

Human-AI Collaboration:

- Emphasizing the augmentation of human capabilities with AI rather than replacement. Collaborative AI systems are designed to work alongside humans, enhancing decision-making and productivity in various fields.

Leading Companies That Are at The Forefront of AI Innovation And Revolutionizing The Field:

1. **Google (Alphabet Inc.)**

   o Through its subsidiary DeepMind and its own Google AI division, Google is a leader in AI research and applications, including advancements in natural language processing (NLP), computer vision, and autonomous systems.

2. **OpenAI**

   o Known for its development of the GPT series, including GPT-4, OpenAI is a prominent player in AI research and development, focusing on creating safe and beneficial AI.

3. **IBM**

   o IBM's Watson platform is a leading AI and machine learning system that offers solutions in healthcare, finance, customer service, and more. IBM is also a key contributor to AI research.

4. **Microsoft**
   - Through its Azure AI platform and research initiatives, Microsoft is a major force in AI. It offers a wide range of AI services and tools for businesses and developers.

5. **Amazon Web Services (AWS)**
   - AWS provides comprehensive AI and machine learning services, including Amazon SageMaker, which helps developers build, train, and deploy machine learning models.

6. **NVIDIA**
   - NVIDIA is a leader in AI hardware and software, known for its GPUs that are widely used in deep learning. The company's CUDA platform and AI frameworks like TensorRT are essential tools in AI development.

7. **Apple**
   - Apple integrates AI across its product line, from Siri to advanced features in iOS and macOS. The company is also heavily involved in AI research and development, particularly in computer vision and NLP.

8. **Facebook (Meta Platforms, Inc.)**
    - Meta invests significantly in AI research through its Facebook AI Research (FAIR) lab, working on projects in areas like computer vision, NLP, and augmented reality.

9. **Baidu**
    - Baidu is a leading AI company in China, focusing on deep learning, NLP, and autonomous driving technologies. Its Baidu AI Cloud offers a range of AI services and solutions.

10. **Tencent**
    - Another Chinese tech giant, Tencent leverages AI across its services, including social media, gaming, and cloud computing. The company is also involved in AI research and applications.

11. **Alibaba**
    - Alibaba's DAMO Academy focuses on AI research and development, particularly in e-commerce, logistics, and cloud computing. Alibaba Cloud provides robust AI solutions for businesses.

12. **Intel**
    - Intel is a key player in AI hardware, developing specialized processors and technologies for AI workloads. The company also invests in AI software and research initiatives.

13. **Tesla**
    - Tesla is at the forefront of AI in autonomous driving. The company's AI efforts are focused on developing self-driving technologies and advanced driver-assistance systems.

14. **Huawei**
    - Huawei is a major contributor to AI research and development, particularly in telecommunications and consumer electronics. Its AI-powered devices and cloud services are widely used.

15. **Salesforce**
    - Through its Einstein AI platform, Salesforce integrates AI into its CRM solutions, providing intelligent insights and automation for sales, marketing, and customer service.

16. **Uber**
    - Uber leverages AI for optimizing its ride-sharing and delivery services. The company is also involved in AI research for autonomous driving and logistics.

17. **Adobe**
    - Adobe integrates AI into its creative and marketing products through its Adobe Sensei platform, enhancing capabilities in image and video editing, digital marketing, and customer experiences.

18. **Zoom**
    - Zoom uses AI to improve video conferencing experiences, including features like virtual backgrounds, noise cancellation, and meeting transcriptions.

19. **Palantir Technologies**
    - Palantir provides AI-powered data analytics platforms for government and commercial clients, focusing on big data analysis, intelligence, and decision-making.

20. **C3.ai**

    - C3.ai offers enterprise AI software for developing, deploying, and operating large-scale AI, IoT, and big data applications, serving industries like energy, healthcare, and manufacturing.

www.ingramcontent.com/pod-product-compliance
Lightning Source LLC
Chambersburg PA
CBHW080435240526
45479CB00016B/1309